MONSTROUS
MONTREAL

by Joyce Markovics

Consultant: Debbie Felton
Professor of Classics
University of Massachusetts
Amherst, Massachusetts

BEARPORT
PUBLISHING

New York, New York

Credits

Cover, © FOTOimage Montreal/Shutterstock and © Evgeniia Litovchenko/Shutterstock; TOC, © Songquan Deng/Shutterstock; 4–5, © Denis Roger/Shutterstock, © Skodonnell/iStock, © Romariolen/Shutterstock, © Baimieng/Shutterstock, and © Zacarias Pereira da Mata/Shutterstock; 6, © KatarzynaBialasiewicz/iStock; 7, © 2018 Google Maps; 8, © tobkatrina/Shutterstock; 9, © KPGA Ltd/Alamy and © janniwet/Shutterstock; 10, © 2016 Google Maps; 11, © McCord Museum; 12–13, © Antoniya G. Kozhuharova/Shutterstock, © Kangah/iStock, © Bertold Werkman/Shutterstock, and © Chakkrit Wiangkham/Shutterstock; 14–15, © Mario Beauregard Beaustock/Alamy; 16, © McCord Museum; 17, © Nina G/Shutterstock; 18L, © Kiril Stanchev/Shutterstock and © Dieter Hawlan/Shutterstock; 18R, © Des Green/Shutterstock; 19, © Lee Brown/Alamy; 20, © Oksana Mizina/Shutterstock; 21, © McCord Museum; 24, © Martin Good/Shutterstock.

Publisher: Kenn Goin
Senior Editor: Joyce Tavolacci
Creative Director: Spencer Brinker
Photo Researcher: Thomas Persano
Cover: Kim Jones

Library of Congress Cataloging-in-Publication Data in process at time of publication (2019)
Library of Congress Control Number: 2018009289
ISBN-13: 978-1-68402-669-2 (library binding)

For more information, write to Bearport Publishing Company, Inc., 45 West 21st Street, Suite 3B, New York, New York 10010. Printed in the United States of America.

10 9 8 7 6 5 4 3 2 1

CONTENTS

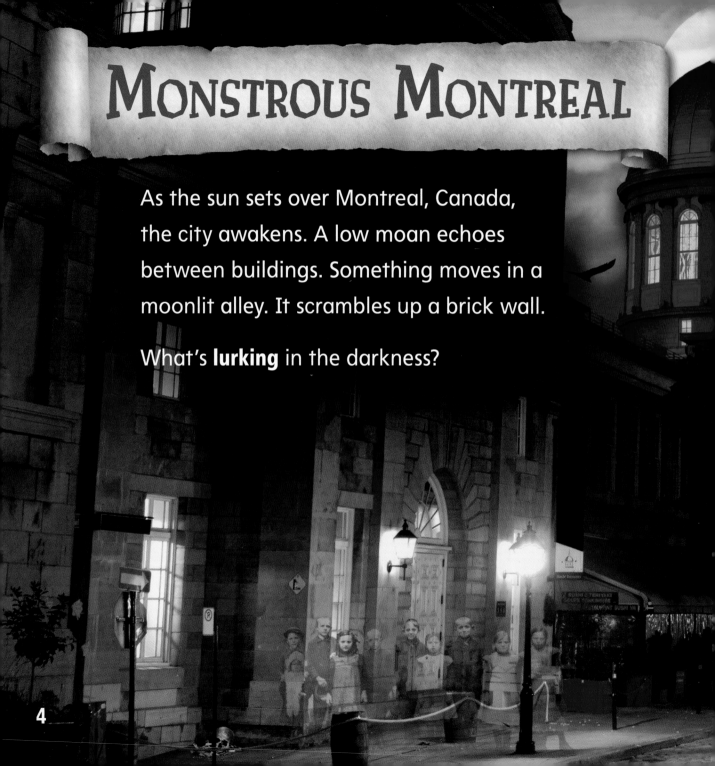

Monstrous Montreal

As the sun sets over Montreal, Canada, the city awakens. A low moan echoes between buildings. Something moves in a moonlit alley. It scrambles up a brick wall.

What's **lurking** in the darkness?

Get ready to read four spine-tingling stories about Montreal. Turn the page . . . if you dare.

FATAL FIRE

Grey Nuns Building, Concordia University

One night, a student jolted awake in her **dormitory** in the Grey Nuns Building. Her heart pounded. She had dreamed about children burning in a fire.

The student had had this same nightmare often. At the time, she didn't know about the building's **tragic** past. . . .

The Grey Nuns Building

In 1918, the Grey Nuns Building was an **orphanage.** One cold February night, a fire broke out. The children were trapped. At least 50 of them died in the blaze.

Do ghostly children haunt the building? Could that explain the student's nightmares?

The scared student finally moved out of the building. Then her nightmares stopped.

Faceless Spirit

Le Cinq nightclub

An old house stands on Mountain Street. For 75 years, it was a **funeral home.** Dead bodies were kept in the building's basement. In 1978, the home was turned into Le Cinq **nightclub**—and a hangout for ghostly guests.

Le Cinq nightclub

The building in the 1930s when it was a funeral home

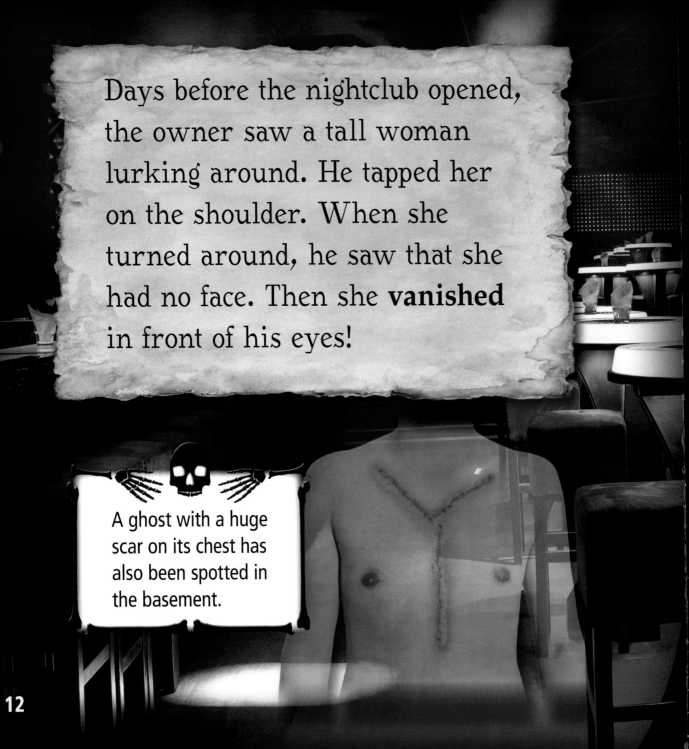

Days before the nightclub opened, the owner saw a tall woman lurking around. He tapped her on the shoulder. When she turned around, he saw that she had no face. Then she **vanished** in front of his eyes!

A ghost with a huge scar on its chest has also been spotted in the basement.

Soon after bumping into the **spirit**, the terrified owner sold the club. However, the faceless ghost has been seen many times since.

THE DEAD UNDERFOOT

Place du Canada

The Place du Canada is a lovely city park. It's filled with flowers and trees. People often sit on benches or stroll around. Little do they know what lies 6 feet (1.8 m) underground.

Place du Canada

HÔTEL THE QUEEN ELIZABETH

15

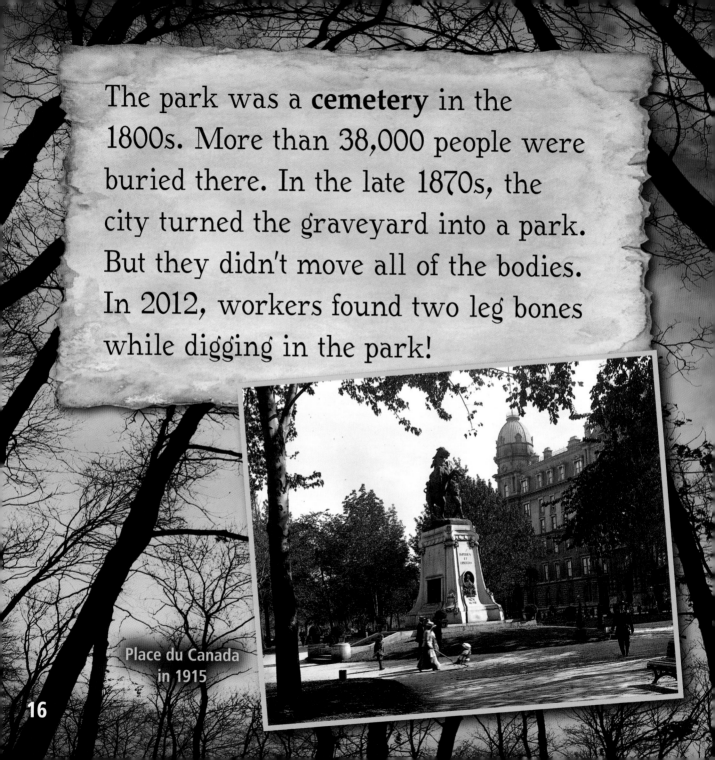

The park was a **cemetery** in the 1800s. More than 38,000 people were buried there. In the late 1870s, the city turned the graveyard into a park. But they didn't move all of the bodies. In 2012, workers found two leg bones while digging in the park!

Place du Canada in 1915

Some of the bodies were moved to a nearby cemetery. However, thousands remain in the park to this day.

THE HAUNTED PAINTING

Royal Victoria Hospital

A painting once hung in the Royal Victoria Hospital. It showed a pretty house in a meadow. **Patients** and staff would stop to admire it. One day, a creepy old woman suddenly appeared in the painting!

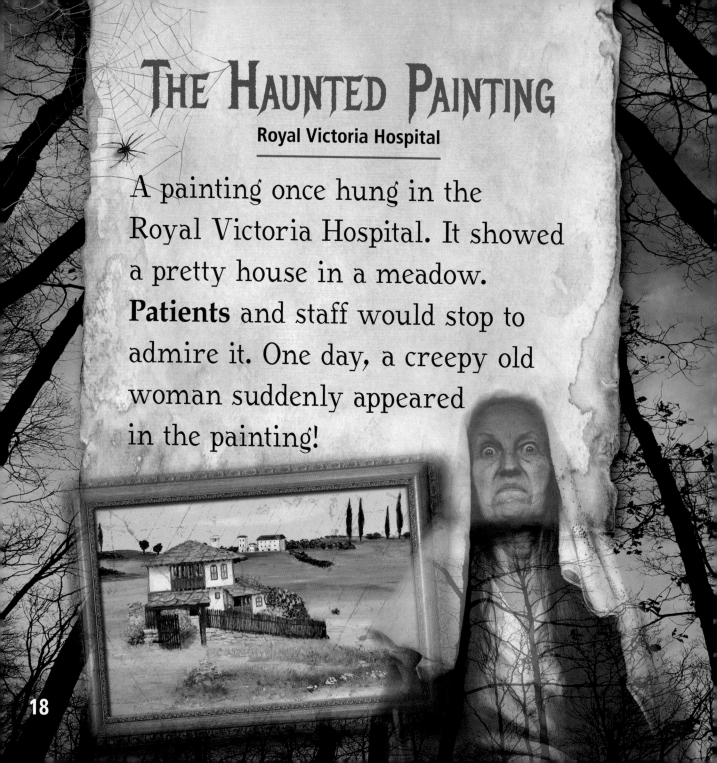

Royal Victoria
Hospital

19

People saw the old woman in different places in the painting. Some said she peeked out of a house window. Others claimed she stepped out of the painting and into the hospital! The spooky painting was finally removed and locked away.

Another scary report tells of patients waking up in unexplained pools of blood in the hospital.

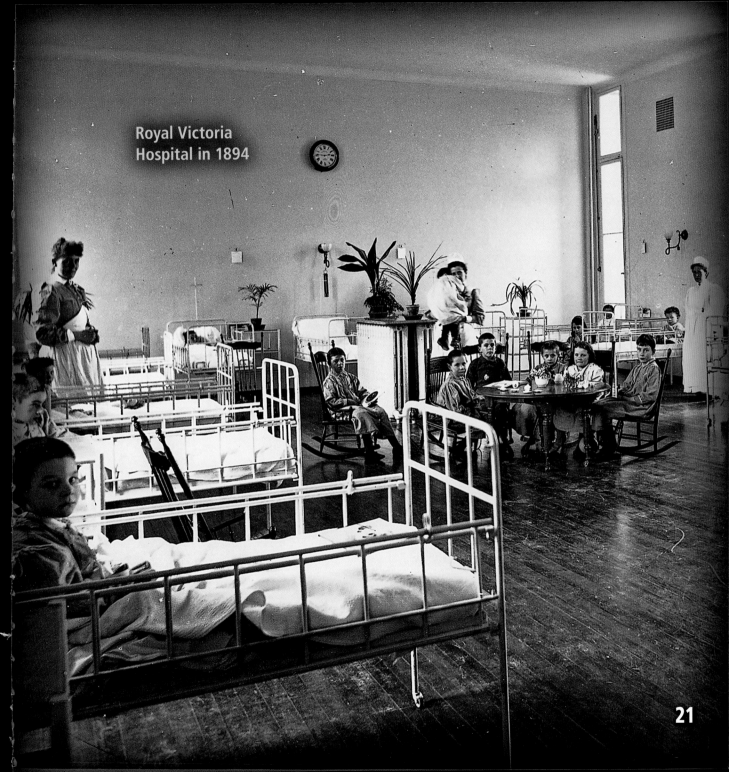

Royal Victoria
Hospital in 1894

Spooky Spots in Montreal

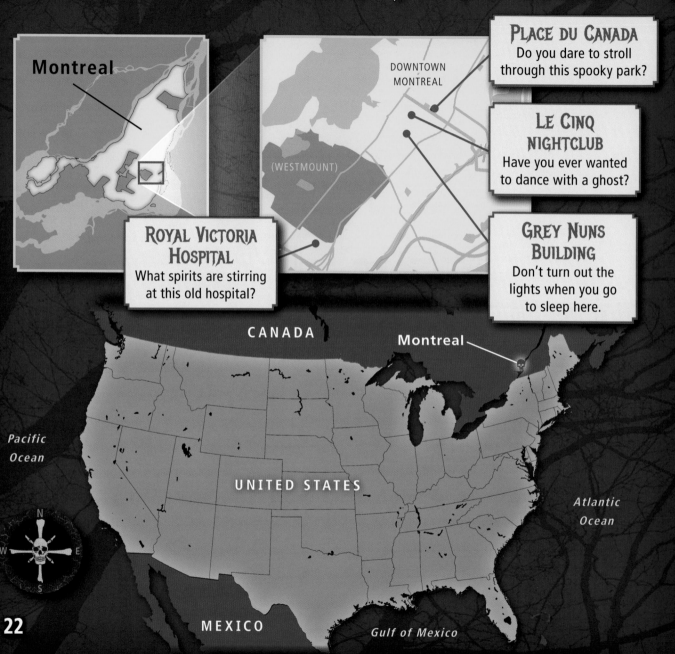

Montreal

DOWNTOWN MONTREAL

(WESTMOUNT)

PLACE DU CANADA
Do you dare to stroll through this spooky park?

LE CINQ NIGHTCLUB
Have you ever wanted to dance with a ghost?

ROYAL VICTORIA HOSPITAL
What spirits are stirring at this old hospital?

GREY NUNS BUILDING
Don't turn out the lights when you go to sleep here.

CANADA

Montreal

UNITED STATES

Pacific Ocean

Atlantic Ocean

MEXICO

Gulf of Mexico

Glossary

cemetery (SEM-uh-ter-ee)
an area of land where dead bodies
are buried

dormitory (DOR-muh-tor-ee)
a building where students live

funeral home (FYOO-nuh-ruhl
HOHM) a building where the dead
are prepared for burial

lurking (LURK-ing) secretly hiding

nightclub (NITE-kluhb) a place of
entertainment open in the evening

orphanage (OR-fuh-nij) a place
where orphans—children without
parents—live and are cared for

patients (PAY-shuhnts) people who
are being treated by a doctor

spirit (SPIHR-it) a supernatural
creature, such as a ghost

tragic (TRAJ-ik) sad or unfortunate

vanished (VAN-ishd) disappeared
suddenly from sight

Index

Read More

Markovics, Joyce. *Chilling Cemeteries (Tiptoe Into Scary Places).* New York: Bearport (2017).

Zullo, Allan. *Haunted Kids: True Ghost Stories.* New York: Scholastic (2000).

Learn More Online

To learn more about monstrous Montreal, visit:
www.bearportpublishing.com/Tiptoe

About the Author

Joyce Markovics is a children's book writer who lives in a 160-year-old house. Chances are a few otherworldly beings live there, too.